How to Improve Communication in your Marriage

~A Pamphlet of Hope~
Doing it God's Way

Lisa Thornton Stillwell

Front Cover Photo Credit: 4774344seanfotosearch.com
Written in Partnership with Point Harbor Church

ISBN-13: 978-0692710678
ISBN-10: 0692710671

Introduction

This pamphlet was written so that it might help you learn how to communicate better in your marriage. Let's face it! Everyone hits those bumps in the road when they have more to say to their spouse than others. It doesn't mean that you don't love them. But if the lack of communication becomes a habit then you might have a more serious problem. I pray that you will take each tip to heart and put it into practice. Your marriage is worth it! Communication is vital to have a happy marriage. You should never use communication as a means to hurt your spouse. Always use words to build them up. Remember, once angry words are spoken you can never get them back. Angry words cut deep and can sometimes have lasting consequences. Well, let's get geared up, open these pages, and find the working strategies to heal our marriages!

Making Marriage Work

Many times we are told that it takes both people to make a marriage work. However; this is certainly not accurate. It takes more than the couple to make a long happy marriage. When two people get married, God must be first. Therefore, it takes three! You see, marriage is a beautiful thing! However, during life's journey of ups and downs communication can be lost along the way. When communication is lost the marital friendship that was once beautiful can now be hurtful. It can leave you with a feeling of helplessness and hopelessness. You might wonder what got you to this place and how to fix it. Has communication been lost in your marriage? What are some signs that communication may be damaged in your marital relationship? Let's explore some real life situations to see if you can relate.

Instead of sitting at the dinner table together like you used to do you are now trying to avoid one another at all odds. You make excuses. I will eat later. You grab a bite at the nearest fast food restaurant and eat on the way home from work. Deep down, this feels all wrong. There was a time that you both would sit at the dinner table and enjoy a pleasant conversation together, but now all you do is stare at your drink. There is no longer any eye contact or longing for affection.

Instead of sleeping in the same bedroom one of you is sleeping on the couch. You make excuses for this as well. I stayed up late and didn't want to wake you. Therefore I decided to crash on the sofa. I was not feeling well, so I do not want you to catch it. I was frightened that it was contagious. You were snoring too bad, and I needed to get a good night sleep. Whatever the excuse you keep falling deeper and deeper away from the real blessing that God intended marriage to be!

Instead of talking you just don't speak at all. You are scared if you do talk that you will not be understood. You fear an argument, so you try to stay busy as much as possible. As soon as you walk in the door from work, you begin to clean, say a few words, and then hurry off to the bedroom to be alone. You also might even get busy talking with the children instead of your spouse. Suddenly, you wonder why you feel so disconnected?

You are happier when you are apart. You feel relieved when you are apart because your spouse cannot keep you from doing the things that you enjoy. You are happy that you do not have to hear their constant criticism while they are away. However, beware! This is no way to improve communication and bring you and your spouse closer together. Being apart means what it says. It means APART. Please remember what the Bible says. What God has joined let nobody separate them! (Mark 10:9) There should be nothing worldly or any person that you allow into your life that can harm your relationship.

If you can relate to one of these scenarios, then you need to do your best to correct the problem before it escalates into something far worse.

Now, let's look at 15 possible ways that you can improve communication.

Stop Avoiding One Another

I know that you are probably not used to it anymore, but learn to be back in the same room, have the same schedule, and share a little bit about your day. When you got married to one another, you became one. This did not mean that you would live separate lives. Again, what God has joined let no one separate. (Mark 10:9) Learn to draw close. If you have been doing things different for a while, then this may take more time than you might like. You may have to gradually let things get back to the way they used to be. Work hard on spending time with one another. If you both have busy lives, try to squeeze in every moment that you can. Even if it is just talking over supper or calling one another on the telephone. Don't be so quick to hang up. Instead of avoiding each other enjoy the company. This is God's will for your marriage.

Never Hold a Grudge

It is vital to learn this when it comes to communication. If you are holding any grudge against your spouse in your heart, you must let it go. Moreover, sometimes the grudges are not over big things. Sometimes it can be over a ton of little things that seem to add up over time. Maybe they did not help you wash the dishes? Maybe he or she fell asleep when you were trying to tell them something important. You felt mistreated and undermined like your feelings did not matter. Perhaps you were ignored the very minute that you walked in the door. Maybe this has been happening over and over again, and now you are finally fed up with the way things are going. You decide that the next time you are going to give them a taste of their own medicine. Give them the cold shoulder and not listen at all. This is never a way to solve a problem. Let the grudges go!

Love Unconditionally

Sadly, this is where many marriages seem to make their mistakes. They decide that they want to tag limitations and conditions on their love. Some of these conditions are I will love you as long as you are making me happy. Happiness cannot be found in marriage. Yes, it can bring you pleasure, but true happiness comes from God Himself. Moreover, communication is hurt when we expect our spouse to meet these expectations. Do not put the responsibility of your happiness on your spouse. It is impossible. NEVER PUT CONDITIONS ON LOVE.

True love loves no matter what. True love loves in spite of what they do. Nothing they could ever do could change how much they are loved. No matter how much they screw up. Wouldn't you rather be in a relationship where you are loved no matter what? When we have this kind of love, we are sharing with our spouse the same kind of love that God has for us. When you have "no limits"

on love communication will improve
tremendously because your marriage partner
knows that no matter what they say or do
you will always be there for them. Above
all, love each other deeply, because love
covers a multitude of sins. (1 Peter 4:8)

Do not Ignore Each Other

Ignoring each other is not the right way to
improve communication. When you ignore
one another, you are stating that you do not
care. If you ignore your spouse enough, they
will get to the point that they no longer want
to talk to you.   Ignoring one another is the
biggest way that you can be disrespected.
Moreover, never turn the volume up on the
television while your spouse is trying to talk
to you. Never try to drown their voice out.
That is one action that hurts deep down to
the core. You must learn to have better
respect than that. Ignoring each other also
does not make a problem go away. It does

not deal with the conflict. Find out how to combat conflicts with the love of Christ.

Listen

Sometimes after a long hard day, your spouse may need to blow off steam. Don't take it personally like they are upset with you. Give them eye to eye contact as you are interested in what they are saying. This will show them that their feelings are important and valued. The Bible says to be quick to listen and slow to speak. There is much wisdom in what the Bible says here. When we are quick to listen and slow to respond, then we are not automatically jumping to conclusions or taking things very personally. Being a good listener is wise.

No Nagging

According to the Bible, it says that it is better to live on the rooftop of a house than for a man to live with a nagging wife. In other words, if you have a need, please don't tell them over and over again what it is. Nagging is not the way to get your husband to listen to you. However, wives sometimes feel like if they do not nag that their husband would never pay them any attention. Wives, this is not the kind of attention that you want to get from your husband. You need to back off and let him give you attention on his own. This is way more real and how God designed things to work. Nagging is never the best form of communication and at times can create bigger distances between you and your spouse. Is that worth it?

Be Honest

It is not healthy to build a marriage on lies. Even little lies can harm your marital communication in more ways than one. The happiest couples are those that are open with one another, and they are not afraid to reveal themselves to the other person. This is one thing that will destroy communication and trust. The Bible says always to tell the truth. It says in the book of John that you shall know the truth and the truth shall set you free. If you have been lying to your spouse, the best thing to do is to start by being honest. If you have sinned by lying then confess your sin and turn away from it. The Bible says If you confess your sins God is faithful and just and will forgive your sins and cleanse you from all unrighteousness. When you continue to lie to your spouse, your dishonesty is destroying trust in your marriage, and you may not even know it.

Remain Approachable

Think about God and how much he loves you. Do you know that you can always approach him about anything that is on your mind? Do you know that he understands you from the inside out? What if every time you went to God, he reminded you about how disappointed he was in you? What if he screamed at you because so many times you acted like you did not love Him? What if ever time you said, God can I have a few minutes of your day and moreover, he stated that he was too busy for you. What if he rolled his eyes at the sound of your voice? What if he was not approachable? What if you just couldn't count on him for anything?

Now think about your marriage partner. Do you think they would feel so much better if they knew that they could come to you about anything? We should learn to look at our spouse as our best friend. Someone we can share the ups and downs of life with. Someone you can approach about anything, and it is always met with understanding.

Control your Emotions

The fruits of the Spirit is love, joy, peace, patience, kindness, goodness, faithfulness, gentleness, and self-control. Do you possess all these fruits in your heart? If not then ask God to help you. Get on your knees beside your bed. If you cannot get on your knees beside your bed to pray then find a quite place to talk with him. Go in your closet, sit down, and shut the door when no one is watching. Jesus will show up, meet your need, and reward you. If you are not controlling your emotions when you talk with your spouse, you are giving the devil a foothold into your marriage. Satan comes to steal, kill, and destroy. Sometimes we like to blame our spouse for our actions, but when it comes down to it, they do not make us react the way that we do. We each have a choice. Just because someone might say something hurtful to us does not mean that we have to say something hurtful back. Two wrongs do not make a right, and that definitely will not bridge the communication gap. Moreover, never go to bed angry. Try to make sure that all your disagreements are resolved. Don't let them carry on over into the next day. Because what starts out as something little, over time, can build into something huge and destroy your marriage. The Bible says don't let the sun do down on your anger. There is much wisdom in that saying. So many couples have gone to bed saying an angry word and come to find out that they wake up and their spouse has taken all their belongings and left. Don't let this happen to you. God did not design marriage so that everyone would get divorced. Marriage was meant to be a lifetime commitment. It was supposed to be a gift to be enjoyed and not something to be endured.

Never Give the Silent Treatment

The silent treatment can be defined as the cold shoulder. It is not to be mistaken for if you can say nothing nice do not say anything at all. These two things are something entirely different. The silent treatment is when you withhold your love and affection from someone because you are mad or things did not quite go your way. If we are to live like Christ, then this is not the way that we should be demonstrating love. When you give someone the cold shoulder or the silent treatment that is belittling them, and that is very hurtful. Sometimes the silent treatment can hurt the person so much that they will not come back to talk to you ever again. It is hard to repair a bridge that you blew completely up with your actions. However; over time you can rebuild it, but it does not always happen overnight. Trust has to be established once again, and the other person needs to see that they are valued and respected as an individual.

Pray Together

Bring your needs before the Lord. God designed marriage, and he is the only one that knows how to fix it. The Bible says where two or three are gathered together in His name that He is there in the midst of them. Make your requests unique to God and be Be honest in your prayers. Don't criticize each other for how you are feeling. Surrender to God your negative feelings so that you both can move forward as a couple. If you are not used to praying together then start off with something small. Pray for your neighbor next door. Then gradually, work your way into praying about other things. God knows what is in your heart. Praying is a beautiful thing that has healed many marriages over the course of time. There is power in prayer.

Soak Yourself in God's Holy Word

Reading God's word is the only true way that you are ever going to grow as a couple. However; getting into a daily Bible reading is not always the easiest thing to do, but it is vital for your relationship and your spiritual well being. Therefore, challenge yourself to get up every morning and read your Bible. Meditate on it before you even start your day. Write down a few Bible verses and stick them in your pocket. Refer to them at lunch time and all throughout the day at work. Let God transform you from the inside out. God is the only person that can change you and make you into the spouse that He would have you to be. I promise you the more you read your Bible and study God's word then you will want to do it more and more. You will begin to wonder how you ever went without it. Reading God's word feeds your soul, and without it, you lack the right spiritual nourishment that you need to be able to function with. God's word is something that you can believe in. It is the only words in this world that will never let you down. People will let you down, and you might as well expect that because they are not perfect. However, God is there twenty-four hours a day and seven days a week. He always has time for you, and he loves you so very much. Listen to what God has to say to you by reading His word. He hears your prayers and the silent cries of your heart so please listen to him.

Set Regular Date Nights

Set aside one night a week to go on a date. It does not matter how many years you have been married. Date nights are crucial and shouldn't stop after marriage. Date nights help to keep the spark in your love life and leave you feeling connected. If you and your spouse have a connection, then it is much harder to break communication. Go out to eat, to a movie, and just do something that you both simply enjoy. If you have small children, then you should find a babysitter. Sometimes it is easier to connect when it is just the two of you. Focus on just the two of you and when you come back after doing that your family will be so much stronger. The Devil, our adversary, is after the family more than anything in this world. He knows that if he has mom and dad, then he has the whole family. He wants to see you fight. He wants children to see mom and dad fight. If you are not communicating, then he knows that your kids are not going to grow up knowing how to talk. Let the healing begin. It is very very important.

Forgive One Another

 If you have been together long enough, you will surely find out that you and your spouse are not perfect. You will discover that you both make mistakes AND because you are human over time, you will unintentionally hurt one another's feelings. The Bible says that we should forgive. Without forgiveness, you will never learn how to communicate in your marriage effectively. The Bible says that we should forgive not just seven times but seven times seventy. This means that we should forgive over and over again. There should be no limit on how many times we should forgive our spouse.

Treat your husband with respect and your wife with understanding. These two things are imperative in a relationship. This is how God designed a man and a woman. If a woman is not respecting her husband communication will suffer. The same is if a man does not understand his wife communication will suffer as well. However; it is a two-way street, but someone is going to have to give in first.

Do not be Prideful

Don't let pride keep you from doing the right thing. Don't let pride make you think that you are perfect. When a person is prideful, they can sometimes find fault more in other than themselves. When people are prideful, they do not want to admit that they have things in their life that they might need to change. Sometimes prideful people even know that they are wrong but just don't want to admit that the other person is right. Proving yourself right often comes with a high price tag. The price entails tearing the person you love down more than anyone else. Pride is a very selfish emotion. It does not care about what the other person is saying or doing. As long as there is pride in a relationship communication by no means will not be successful. To have healthy communication in your marriage, you must get rid of your prideful heart. Surrender this negative emotion to the Lord. Ask him to replace pride with a spirit of understanding.Pride is so deceitful. Therefore, if you are in an argument with your spouse, Don't wait for the other person to say sorry first. Come out and be the first one that says it.

When pride comes, then comes disgrace, but with humility comes wisdom. (Proverbs 11:2)

One's pride will bring him low, but who is lowly in spirit will obtain honor.

Don't let the center of your conversations every day be about the bills, cleaning the house, taking care of the children. Don't let the first thing that comes out of your mouth be everything that needs to be done throughout the day. When you are looking for good communication when you come home from work why not walk up to your partner and give them a hug. Maybe you can just say that it is nice to be home. Thank them if they have supper made. Give your worries to God on the way home from work so that when you get home, you are not bombarding your spouse with a thousand different things that only God can handle. If you bombard your spouse with so many things that they already know needs to be done, you are going to wind up pushing them away. Although this stuff needs to be discussed if you overtalk it then it can be quite draining. It can drain the person you love from their energy because it creates stress in a round about way. They will begin to shy away when you first walk through the door when you get home from work because they think "all you seem to like" is someone that is there to take care of things around the house versus actually being a marriage partner. There is a difference between being marriage partners and roommates.

Moreover, when married people talk more

about the transactions of the day then they are falling victim to acting more like roommates and not enjoying the actual marital gift that God has given them, and that is each other.

Don't hold past mistakes against your spouse. The Bible says that once we forgive, then we should throw that thing away. Don't look at your spouse and bring up every bad thing that they have ever done. The Bible says in 1 Corinthians 13: 4-6 that this is love.

Love is patient; love is kind. It does not envy; it does not boast, it is not proud. It is not rude; it is not self-seeking, it is not easily angered, it keeps no record of wrongs. Love does not delight in evil but rejoices with the truth. It always protects, always trusts, always hopes, and always perseveres.

Let's look further into God's definition of love.

Love is patient. This means that you should try your best to never lose your patience with you spouse. When you lose your patience with the one that you love so very much, you are selfish. Selfishness is not the kind of life that God desires for you to have. He wants you to be unselfish. Unselfishness is one of the fruits of the Holy Spirit. Moreover, it is very very important to put our spouses need before our own. The Bible says to look out for the interest of others. When you are patient, you are honestly doing that. When you are patient, you also set the stage for communication. It is easier to talk to someone that is calm versus someone that is going to blow their top at any moment.

Love is kind. You can show kindness in the things you do for your spouse. You might be wondering what you can do? Husbands, maybe one night you could wash the dishes for no reason at all. Perhaps you could set the coffee pot in the morning or crank the car on a winter day, so it is warm when she climbs into the car to go to work. Maybe you can help the kids with all their homework so you wife can have extra time to herself. Give her a little money that she can spend on just her. Maybe she would like to get her hair done, spend a day at the beach, or just go hang out with a friend to eat at their favorite restaurant. Wives, perhaps you could cook your husband's favorite for supper and just let him spend the rest of the evening unwinding from his long day. You might find that this will go a long way when it comes to communicating properly. Just showing random acts of kindness without expecting anything in return. Give up something that you would like to do just so that you can be with your spouse.

It does not envy. This means that there is no room for jealousy. Yes, we should desire our spouse for ourselves. We should have eyes for them and them only. However; we should not be jealous to the point where we want to know where they have been ever second of every day. We should not want them to explain it to us because we are jealous. This is not healthy communication. Your spouse should have no problem telling you about their day they should never be asked out of jealousy or mistreated because of it. The Bible says that jealousy and selfish ambition is a huge destroyer of relationships. However, if you harbor bitter envy and selfish ambition in your hearts, do not boast about it or deny the truth. Such wisdom does not come down from Heaven but is earthly, unspiritual, of the devil. For where you have envy and selfish ambition, there you find disorder and every evil practice. James 3: 14-16

So you need to turn from that kind of wisdom and seek the wisdom that comes from Heaven. The wisdom that comes from Heaven is first of all pure, then peace-loving, considerate, submissive, full of mercy and good fruit, impartial and sincere. Peacemakers who sow in peace raise a harvest of righteousness. James 3:17-19

It keeps no record of wrongs. This means that every time you get into an argument you are not throwing up in your marriage partners face all the mistakes they did the last time you were in an argument. This will only make them feel worse and also hurt the means of communication Also, and what about your marriage partner's life before Christ? Should you throw that up in his face? Of course not! When the Bible talks about keeping no record of wrongs, it means not keeping any records of wrong at all. We should not regularly throw anyone's past up in their face no matter how ugly it looks. Why would we want to do that? That is not the kind of love that Jesus teaches us that we should have. Moreover, no wrong is bigger than the next wrong. The Bible tells us that sin is a sin. It is all level at the cross, and no sin is greater than the other. True love keeps no records of wrongs.

It does not delight in evil. This means that you do no take pleasure in destroying one another. You can destroy one another in so many different ways. Moreover, truthfully, you can take pleasure in doing that.

However, there is nothing good that will come out of it. You do not need to have the attitude that well, he hurt me, so then I will hurt him.

It rejoices with the truth. It always protects, trusts, hopes and perseveres. Think about this for a minute. Wouldn't this set the tone for a good marriage? Love rejoices with the truth! Love protects! Love will trust! Love will hope! Love will persevere. When love persists, it does not give up. It keeps on until it finds a resolution. There will not always be happy times in a marriage. There will be times when you may feel like quitting, but according to this Bible verse if you have real love you are willing to do anything for it!

It keeps no record of wrongs. It does not rejoice in evil but always rejoices in the truth.

Give one another your undivided attention when talking. This means turn off the television, your cell phones, or any other distraction. When your attention is diverted, it is even harder to communicate.Plus it makes the other person at times feel like you are not paying attention and what they are saying is not important.

Call one another in the middle of the day just to say hello. It could be that you could call your spouse on the way home from work of you could send a text for no reason at all other than to only say I love you. You would be surprised at how this simple gesture might help you in this endeavor.

Now let's close with a word of prayer for our marriages!

Dear Lord,

Thank you for the gift of marriage. Thank you for the wonderful person that you have given to me to love and cherish for the rest of my life. Lord, help us on this journey. Help us be a stronger couple. May we bear with one another in love and forgiveness just like you do for us on a day to day basis. Help us grow in our communication to one another without saying hurtful words that can leave permanent scars. Help us only say words that will build one another up instead of tearing them down. Lord, this is your special blessing to me. I love my partner and thank you for bringing my spouse into my life.

In Jesus Name, Amen.

Made in the USA
Las Vegas, NV
04 July 2025

24430525R00021